B
REA

• FROM BRF •

FOR THE
EASTER SEASON

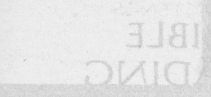

Text copyright © BRF 2002

Published by
The Bible Reading Fellowship
First Floor, Elsfield Hall
15–17 Elsfield Way, Oxford OX2 8FG
ISBN 1 84101 309 9

First published 2002
10 9 8 7 6 5 4 3 2 1 0
All rights reserved

Printed and bound in Great Britain by
Omnia Books Limited, Glasgow

CONTENTS

GENERAL INTRODUCTION

Welcome to the Easter edition of BRF's Bible reading sampler. We think you'll find something to enjoy here, whether it's a taste of our regular Bible reading notes, an extract from one of our *People's Bible Commentary volumes*, or simply finding out more about the range of publications that we produce.

At BRF we are passionate about helping people grow in personal Bible reading and prayer, as well as in being a member of the Christian Church. By reading the Bible, we grow in the knowledge of how our faith fits together, and this nurtures our prayer life, both as individuals and as worshipping communities. And reading with the help of insightful comment from others can help us get deeper into God's word, challenge our assumptions and bring us fresh insights into familiar passages.

Naomi Starkey

Naomi Starkey
Managing Editor, Bible reading notes

New Daylight

New Daylight is ideal for those looking for a devotional approach to reading and understanding the Bible. Each issue covers four months of daily Bible readings and reflection from a regular team of contributors, who have represented a stimulating mix of church backgrounds, from Baptist to Anglican Franciscan. Each day's reading provides a Bible passage (text included), helpful comment and prayer or thought for reflection. In *New Daylight* the Sundays and special festivals from the Church calendar are noted on the relevant days, offering a chance to get acquainted with the rich traditions of the Christian year. Our *New Daylight* extract is from the January–April 2002 notes, and the comment is written by Helen Julian CSF, Guardian of St Francis Convent in Somerset and author of *Living the Gospel* (BRF, 2001).

Wisdom to choose

To what then will I compare the people of this generation, and what are they like? They are like children sitting in the marketplace and calling to one another, 'We played the flute for you, and you did not dance; we wailed, and you did not weep.' For John the Baptist has come eating no bread and drinking no wine, and you say, 'He has a demon'; the Son of Man has come eating and drinking, and you say, 'Look, a glutton and a drunkard, a friend of tax-collectors and sinners!' Nevertheless, wisdom is vindicated by all her children.

'Some people are never satisfied', you can almost hear Jesus say in exasperation. He has just healed the centurion's slave, and the widow of Nain's son. He has named John the Baptist as a great prophet and God's messenger, preparing the way for the Messiah. Yet, many of the religious people, the Pharisees and the lawyers, refuse to accept either John or Jesus. They are, says Jesus, like spoilt, sulky children, who won't join in with the game their friends are playing, because it's always the wrong game.

So, John comes, living an ascetic life, living in the wilderness and fasting, and they accuse him of being possessed. Jesus comes, eating and drinking, often with the less respectable people, and they accuse him of being a greedy drunkard. God, though, has sent both John and Jesus. Each is honouring God in the way he lives, and each has his own followers.

Certainly Jesus had fasted and would fast again, but, for now, it was right to feast, to share meals with those who were not usually invited to feasts. John's ministry and Jesus' ministry complement each other, yet each is criticized for not doing what the other does.

'For everything there is a season… a time to mourn, and a time to dance' (Ecclesiastes 3:1, 4). We need the wisdom to know what is right for this season and time. Jesus, the wisdom of God (1 Corinthians 1:24), leads his children so we know when it is time to fast or to feast, to mourn or to dance.

Sunday Reflection

Jesus, wisdom of God, make me sensitive to your leading and ready to follow wholeheartedly.

HJ CSF

Generous God

Ho, everyone who thirsts, come to the waters; and you that have no money, come, buy and eat! Come, buy wine and milk without money and without price. Why do you spend your money for that which is not bread, and your labour for that which does not satisfy? Listen carefully to me, and eat what is good, and delight yourselves in rich food. Incline your ear, and come to me; listen, so that you may live.

Visiting India, I was struck by the number of people selling water by the roadside. A very small sum bought a glass of water, with a squeeze of lime. Imagine having to buy your water by the glassful or, even worse, being too poor to pay even the tiny price of a drink? Especially in a hot country, that really is being in want.

In this parable, God is a water seller like no other. The familiar cry, drawing attention to what he has to sell, is transformed. This water seller is giving away his stock free to anyone who needs it. His stock is not only water, but also bread, and not only bread and water, the necessities of life, but also wine and milk, the luxuries.

In Isaiah's parable, God is not only the street seller, but also the rich benefactor. Someone wishing to be generous would buy up the entire stock of a water-carrier or a baker and order him to distribute it free. God does this not once but continuously. His generosity is unmatched.

There is still more. Not content with supplying free both the necessities of life and the luxuries, he goes on to promise the gift of life itself. Bread and water, wine and milk, may be necessary and pleasurable, but they are not enough. If all our energies are focused on them and what they stand for, we will ultimately not be satisfied. Only in coming to God and listening to his word—the Word, Jesus—will we receive the greatest gift of our generous God: 'I came that they may have life, and have it abundantly' (John 10:10).

Reflection

On what do I spend my money and my labour?

HJ CSF

Show me

Blow the trumpet in Zion; sound the alarm on my holy mountain! Let all the inhabitants of the land tremble, for the day of the Lord is coming, it is near... a great and powerful army comes... Yet even now, says the Lord, return to me with all your heart, with fasting, with weeping, and with mourning; rend your hearts and not your clothing. Return to the Lord, your God, for he is gracious and merciful, slow to anger, and abounding in steadfast love, and relents from punishing. Who knows whether he will not turn and relent, and leave a blessing behind him, a grain offering and a drink offering for the Lord, your God?

'Don't talk of love, show me,' sang Eliza Doolittle in *My Fair Lady*. Here are God's people, facing a great calamity, a mighty army advancing on them, and this is God's doing—'the day of the Lord is coming'. Recognizing this, the people want to demonstrate to God their sorrow for their sins, their unfaithfulness, everything that has brought this day on them. Just talking about it won't do. Like Eliza Doolittle, God wants something more concrete. Fasting and weeping and mourning are ways of showing God their love and sorrow. They back up the words and strengthen them.

But even such dramatic action, though more effective than words alone, is not enough. The call is to repent 'with all your heart'. For the Hebrews, this did not necessarily mean 'with all your feeling'.

The heart represented intellect and will as much as emotions, so perhaps 'with all your heart' could be translated as 'with purpose and resolve'. The heart must also be torn, broken, as mourners tore their clothes as a sign of grief.

The heart, broken open, with a real resolution to change, can then truly turn, return, repent and come back into a relationship with the gracious and merciful God. This return is celebrated with feasting, grain and drink offerings to God, who waits with steadfast love to feast with his people.

Reflection

What authentic ways can I find of showing God my penitence for sin?

HJ CSF

Glory to God

And whenever you fast, do not look dismal, like the hypocrites, for they disfigure their faces so as to show others that they are fasting. Truly I tell you, they have received their reward. But when you fast, put oil on your head and wash your face, so that your fasting may be seen not by others but by your Father who is in secret; and your Father who sees in secret will reward you.

The key word here is 'whenever'. Jesus takes it for granted that his disciples will give alms, pray and fast and here he tells them how to go about these practices. 'How to' is only the beginning, though—far more important, and far more demanding, is 'why'.

'Beware of practising your piety before others in order to be seen by them…' (6:1). The almsgiver should not be accompanied down the street by a servant blowing a trumpet. The one who prays should go into their room and shut the door. When Jesus' disciples fast, it should be as a personal act of devotion between them and God. No one else should be able to tell. They should look and act as they normally do.

Does this contradict what Jesus said just a little earlier in the Sermon on the Mount—'Let your light shine before others, so that they may see your good works' (5:16)? No, because, again, the motivation is all-important. Verse 16 goes on to say 'and give glory to your Father in heaven'. God must be the focus of almsgiving, prayer and fasting and God's reward is the only one the disciples long for. It's a good test of our Lent resolutions this Ash Wednesday.

Our natural human tendency to want others to think well of us is a problem for the spiritual life. It makes us self-conscious, aware of being seen. The great saints, Francis among them, seem to have escaped this. Francis responded directly to God, praying, singing, dancing, weeping, fasting or feasting. He was so intoxicated with God that he was oblivious of others' opinions of him. His eyes were fixed on God and God's was all the glory.

Prayer

God of glory, help me to fix my eyes only on you.

HJ CSF

9

Hungry for God

There was also a prophet, Anna the daughter of Phanuel, of the tribe of Asher. She was of a great age, having lived with her husband for seven years after her marriage, then as a widow to the age of 84. She never left the temple but worshipped there with fasting and prayer night and day. At that moment she came, and began to praise God and to speak about the child to all who were looking for the redemption of Jerusalem.

'She's never out of the church' may be a compliment or rather less than one. We may perhaps think of a lonely old woman, with no life of her own. Anna, however, who 'never left the temple', is not one of those.

Only seven women in the whole of the Old Testament are named as prophets. Anna's long life of worship in the temple in Jerusalem—the centre of the world for God's people—made her especially sensitive to the signs of God's presence. Like Simeon, she had waited faithfully for the coming of the Messiah. So, when the child Jesus was brought into the temple, she recognized him and knew that this was cause for rejoicing.

Her worship included both prayer and fasting and, in the scriptures, these two usually belong together. Fasting from food in order to focus more completely on God has a long pedigree. Of course, it isn't automatically successful. I have a friend who became so desperate for chocolate while on a fasting retreat that he walked eight miles over mountain paths to buy a bar. 'It was all that was good in the universe,' he recalled. Fasting is not an automatic passport to opening up in us a hunger for God. Rather, it may make it humiliatingly clear where our hunger really lies.

Perhaps Anna, too, found it hard in the beginning. However, she persevered, perhaps for as long as 60 years, and, in the end, her hunger was satisfied. Like Simeon, her eyes saw God's salvation and her soul rejoiced.

Reflection

What am I hungry for?
How might fasting, from food or something else, help me to focus more on God this Lent?

HJ CSF

True fasting

Is not this the fast that I choose: to loose the bonds of injustice, to undo the thongs of the yoke, to let the oppressed go free, and to break every yoke? Is it not to share your bread with the hungry, and bring the homeless poor into your house; when you see the naked, to cover them, and not to hide yourself from your own kin? Then your light shall break forth like the dawn, and your healing shall spring up quickly.

My mother recalls that my sister and I would burst in from school saying, 'Do you know, it's not fair', before we'd even taken our coats off. Then would follow some saga of injustice. The instinct for fair play is a very deep one.

God's people think that he isn't treating them fairly. Just before this passage, they are complaining, 'Why do we fast, but you do not see? Why humble ourselves, but you do not notice?' (v. 3). We are doing all the right things, God. Why are you not rewarding us as we deserve?

God's reply is devastating. Your fasting is worthless if it is accompanied by oppression, quarrelling and violence (vv. 3–4). Fasting like this is only an outward show, an empty ritual.

Then God details what must accompany fasting if it is to be pleasing to him. Justice, liberation, compassion and care for neighbour are what God chooses. These are what please

him, these are what will cause him to hear his people when they call to him.

The prophets call their hearers to 'do justice, and to love kindness' (Micah 6:8). God cares passionately about justice, but we cannot bargain our way into his favour with our fasting or our beautiful services or our long prayers. These have their place, but God looks for justice and compassion, expressed in the very concrete details of our lives, as well.

Prayer

Merciful God, you loose the bonds of injustice and let the oppressed go free: give us the will to share our bread with the hungry and give shelter to the homeless poor, for thus your glory shall be revealed, through Jesus Christ our Lord. Amen

HJ CSF

The feast of the Kingdom

He said also to the one who had invited him, 'When you give a luncheon or a dinner, do not invite your friends or your brothers or your relatives or rich neighbours, in case they may invite you in return, and you would be repaid. But when you give a banquet, invite the poor, the crippled, the lame, and the blind. And you will be blessed, because they cannot repay you, for you will be repaid at the resurrection of the righteous.'

When I moved to the East End of London, I knew what kind of church I wanted to join. I would look for somewhere fairly large and successful where, for a time, I could just sidle in and out and not be asked to do anything. I ended up in a tiny congregation, at that time without a priest, where I was immediately pressed into service, but in the end I was grateful.

Although small, the congregation came from an amazing range of backgrounds. On an average Sunday, there would be traditional working-class East Enders, a retired teacher or two from the leafier suburbs, me from Scotland, two or three older people from the Caribbean, a young family from the Far East, perhaps a Latin American. The priest who soon came to care for the parish was Anglo-Indian. I used to look around at the Eucharist and think, 'This is what the Kingdom looks like.' People from all classes and ages and all parts of the world, united by nothing at all except their desire to worship God.

This is one of Jesus' parables of the Kingdom. The feast of the Kingdom is not like most of our parties—a time to enjoy our friends or perhaps impress our neighbours or colleagues, knowing that next it will be their turn to invite us. The feast of the Kingdom is, as theological commentator Dennis McBride says, for 'people who need food because they are hungry, who need company because they are outcast, who need rejoicing because they know sadness, who need sharing because they are isolated in their sickness'.

Reflection

What would it mean in my life and in my church to follow Jesus' advice to his host?

HJ CSF

Bread in the wilderness

Then Jesus was led up by the Spirit into the wilderness to be tempted by the devil. He fasted for 40 days and 40 nights, and afterwards he was famished. The tempter came and said to him, 'If you are the Son of God, command these stones to become loaves of bread.' But he answered, 'It is written, "One does not live by bread alone, but by every word that comes from the mouth of God."'

This is a story full of echoes. The wilderness, the number 40, stones and bread—all take the reader back to the Old Testament. The voice of the tempter takes Jesus back to the voice at his baptism—'This is my Son, the Beloved' (Matthew 3:17). Jesus goes into the wilderness as the people of Israel did after their liberation from Egypt (Deuteronomy 8:2), and fasts for 40 days, as did both Moses (Exodus 34:28) and Elijah (1 Kings 19:8). For Jesus, as for these others, it is a time of testing—'testing you to know what was in your heart' (Deuteronomy 8:2). The people of Israel failed the test. They doubted God, rebelled against Moses, complained about the food that God provided and even regretted their liberation from slavery.

Jesus does not fail despite all this. He neither takes on the tempter in his own newly realized power, nor does he despair of God's help. He looks back into the tradition out of which he comes and draws from it words to express his trust in God, words from Deuteronomy 8.

William Barclay says, 'We are tempted through our gifts.' It's a sobering thought. We are accustomed to thinking of our weaknesses as places where we may face temptation, but our strengths and gifts can tempt us to the wrong sort of autonomy. The Devil seems to taunt Jesus: 'If you are the Son of God'—prove it to me. Jesus does prove it, but not in a show of power. His obedience to the word of God is a better proof than that. It is also his bread: 'My food is to do the will of him who sent me' (John 4:34).

Sunday Reflection

Where do my gifts lead me into temptation?

HJ CSF

The king's feast

O Lord, you are my God; I will exalt you, I will praise your name; for you have done wonderful things... For you have been a refuge to the poor, a refuge to the needy in their distress... On this mountain the Lord of hosts will make for all peoples a feast of rich food, a feast of well-matured wines, of rich food filled with marrow, of well-matured wines strained clear. And he will destroy on this mountain the shroud that is cast over all peoples, the sheet that is spread over all nations; he will swallow up death for ever.

Perhaps it isn't today's idea of a healthy diet, but the feast of 'rich food, filled with marrow' and the best wines were the caviar and Champagne of their day. This is a description of a coronation banquet, the celebration of the enthronement of God as king. He will reign 'on Mount Zion and in Jerusalem' (Isaiah 24:23) and his reign marks the final defeat of death. Unlike many of the kings of the time, he is a king who brings liberation, who is on the side of the poor, so his coronation banquet is open to everyone, not just the rich and powerful.

St Francis called himself 'the herald of the great king'. He went about preaching the gospel, depending on others to supply his needs. One day, he and Brother Masseo went out to beg. Masseo, who was tall and good-looking, was given many good pieces of bread, even whole loaves. Francis, however, small and ragged, received only a few scraps, ends of loaves, dry and unappetizing. They met outside the town at a fountain to eat. Masseo was aware of how little they had—no plates, knives, tablecloth, servants—but Francis was joyful and praised God for his provision. 'We have this bread as a gift,' he said, 'and water to drink, and a stone by the fountain as our table. Everything is given by God, and so it is a great treasure.'

Rich food and the best wines or bread and water—where God is acknowledged as the giver, everything is feast.

Prayer

Generous God, help me to feast on your gifts today.

HJ CSF

Us and them

If you remove the yoke from among you, the pointing of the finger, the speaking of evil, if you offer your food to the hungry and satisfy the needs of the afflicted, then your light shall rise in the darkness and your gloom be like the noonday. The Lord will guide you continually, and satisfy your needs in parched places, and make your bones strong; and you shall be like a watered garden, like a spring of water, whose waters never fail.

Fasting from food can leave us feeling empty, hungry, for a short time, but the fast ends and once again we can satisfy our hunger. Some hungers, though, can only be satisfied at the expense of others. Our fast from these should be permanent.

'The pointing of the finger, the speaking of evil'—a graphic description of the natural human tendency to divide our world into 'us' and 'them'. Then 'they' can be blamed, even made scapegoats, for the problems we perceive. This can nourish 'us'—we define our identity in opposition to 'them' and feel superior and secure, it builds us up.

God's people always wrestled with this temptation. They had been chosen by God, they had the Law—surely they were superior to the nations around them because of this? The prophets had constantly to remind them that their calling to be God's people was not because they deserved it, but purely because of God's covenant love. Increasingly, they also spoke of God's desire for all the people of the world to come within this covenant.

Gratitude, trust in God and a desire to serve others, not superiority and separation, were the appropriate responses to God's choice of his people. If they fasted from the easy satisfaction of 'us' and 'them', then God would supply their real needs. He would always be with them to guide them and would build up their strength. Their dry places, their thirst, would be reliably watered and their darkness turned to light.

Prayer

Covenant God, teach me to satisfy my hungers only in knowing and serving you. Amen

HJ CSF

Going beyond ourselves

Now in the church at Antioch there were prophets and teachers: Barnabas, Simeon who was called Niger, Lucius of Cyrene, Manaen a member of the court of Herod the ruler, and Saul. While they were worshipping the Lord and fasting, the Holy Spirit said, 'Set apart for me Barnabas and Saul for the work to which I have called them.' Then after fasting and praying, they laid their hands on them and sent them off.

I wonder if Barnabas and Saul wanted to be 'sent off'? Perhaps they were very happy at Antioch. They had been there for a year and the church was growing. They had a recognized role there, numbered among the prophets and teachers. Setting off on a missionary journey round the Eastern Mediterranean may have been the last thing on their minds.

God, however, had other ideas. He used a time of worship and fasting to speak to the church. Fasting has often been used along with prayer to help in discerning God's will and making decisions. Learning that it's possible to do without something that is usually central to life can have a very liberating effect. We begin thinking, 'I couldn't survive without…' but discover that 'actually I can'. That can free us to wonder what else might be possible.

Doing something new and challenging can have the same effect. I always hated sport at school and would have said, 'I'm no good at that sort of thing', but I now practise aikido, a martial art. Every time I pass a grading and get my new coloured belt I'm amazed to find myself doing this. It challenges me in other areas where I might want to say, 'I'm no good at that sort of thing.'

Perhaps this is why firewalking and other apparently impossible feats can have such a transformative effect. As Christians, we draw not only on our own as yet unrecognized resources, but on God's, whose Holy Spirit is always surprising us and challenging us to move beyond the safe and the known, 'For nothing will be impossible with God' (Luke 1:37).

Prayer

God of the impossible, lead me beyond myself into your future.

HJ CSF

Excuses, excuses

Then Jesus said to him, 'Someone gave a great dinner... he sent his slave to say... "Come, for everything is ready now." But they all alike began to make excuses. The first said to him, "I have bought a piece of land, and I must go out and see it; please accept my apologies." Another said, "I have bought five yoke of oxen, and I am going to try them out; please accept my apologies." Another said, "I have just been married, and therefore I cannot come." So the slave returned and reported this... Then the owner of the house became angry and said to the slave, "Go out... and bring in the poor, the crippled, the blind and the lame... so that my house may be filled."'

The slave had already come round once, to announce the feast, and those invited had given their acceptance. Now the feast was ready and he was sent round again to tell them that it was time to come. Only important people were treated like this. However, even though the host had done everything that he should, each guest now had something more important to do. They put their own activities first and so insulted the host by going back on their acceptance.

So the host sends to ask others—the unimportant and those not usually invited to feasts. Only the physically whole could participate fully in Jewish worship, but here the blind and the lame are invited along with everyone else.

No one is excluded from the feast of the Kingdom except by their own choice. God is the host, who will not start the feast until his house is filled with willing guests. When those first invited refused, he could have simply enjoyed the feast on his own or, in anger, cancelled it altogether, but he does not. God wants company at his table, where the feast is always ready.

It's easy to put off responding to God's gracious invitation. Other things seem more urgent and surely God will go on inviting? Yes, God's patience far outruns our procrastination, but each invitation is for 'now' and will not come again. Today's feast will not still be available tomorrow.

Reflection

What excuses do I use to avoid sitting down to feast with God?

HJ CSF

17

Bought at a price

'All things are lawful for me', but not all things are beneficial. 'All things are lawful for me', but I will not be dominated by anything. 'Food is meant for the stomach and the stomach for food', and God will destroy both one and the other. The body is meant not for fornication but for the Lord, and the Lord for the body. And God raised the Lord and will also raise us by his power… Or do you not know that your body is a temple of the Holy Spirit within you, which you have from God, and that you are not your own? For you were bought with a price; therefore glorify God in your body.

Paul has often been used to support a misunderstanding of Christianity, which denigrates and devalues the body. His opposition of 'spirit' and 'flesh' (Romans 8:1–13, Galatians 5:16–25) has been used to support a negative view of the physical. The less attention given to the body the better, so fasting and other harsh treatment are virtuous.

This passage is a corrective to that. The body is 'a temple of the Holy Spirit' and so is to be treated with respect, as a place in which God can be glorified as much as in our mind or heart or spirit. Fasting may be a means of doing this, but so may eating sensibly and taking appropriate exercise.

What Paul does warn against is being 'dominated by anything'. Lent is a good opportunity to examine ourselves —what do I believe I cannot do without? It may be food or, more likely, particular kinds of food (not many people are addicted to lettuce). It may equally be television, surfing the Internet, alcohol, shopping, constant background music, a particular relationship. None are bad in themselves—'all things are lawful'—but if they dominate my life, then they are no longer beneficial.

Fasting from anything that has too high a place in my priorities could be a way of returning God to the centre of my life, acknowledging that I am not my own.

Prayer

Lord, help me to remember that I belong to you and let me seek your glory in all that I do.

HJ CSF

An 'in between' time

Now John's disciples and the Pharisees were fasting; and people came and said to him [Jesus], 'Why do John's disciples and the disciples of the Pharisees fast, but your disciples do not fast?' Jesus said to them, 'The wedding guests cannot fast while the bridegroom is with them, can they? As long as they have the bridegroom with them, they cannot fast. The days will come when the bridegroom is taken away from them, and then they will fast on that day.'

John's disciples and the Pharisees and their disciples were still waiting, waiting for the coming of the Messiah. They were still in the 'in between' time, between the promise and its fulfilment. It was not yet time for the feast.

Jesus' disciples, even at this early stage in the Gospel, however, have come to believe that he is the Messiah, the promised one. For them, there is ample cause for celebration and so fasting would be as inappropriate as it would be at a wedding.

The time will come when the bridegroom will leave them and then, Jesus recognizes, the time of feasting will be over. At the Last Supper, keeping the Passover with his disciples, he vowed to abstain until the coming of the Kingdom (Luke 22:14–18).

So, where are we now? Should we fast or feast? The wedding has taken place, but the bridegroom is no longer with us. We are in another 'in between' time. With the Passion and resurrection of Jesus, the reign of sin is over and the Kingdom has begun, so we can feast. However, the final victory has not yet been realized, so there is still cause for fasting.

In the eucharist, both these perspectives are present. The broken bread and wine, outpoured, look back to Jesus' broken body and the blood he poured out on the cross. A meal shared with friends gathered round a table looks forward to the banquet of the Kingdom, the final celebration of redemption and liberation at the end of the age.

In the space between the 'now' and the 'not yet' of the Kingdom we can both fast and feast.

Prayer

Help me to live creatively in the now, but not lose sight of the 'not yet'.

HJ CSF

Guidelines

Guidelines is a unique Bible reading resource that offers four months of in-depth study written by leading scholars. Contributors are drawn from around the world as well as the UK, and represent a stimulating and thought-provoking breadth of Christian tradition. Instead of dated daily readings, *Guidelines* provides weekly units, broken into at least six sections, plus an introduction giving context for the passage, and a final section of points for thought and prayer. On any day you can read as many or as few sections as you wish. As well as a copy of *Guidelines*, you will need a Bible, as the passage is not included. The *Guidelines* extract in this sampler is by John Goldingay who teaches Old Testament at Fuller Theological Seminary in California.

Ecclesiastes

1 The pointlessness of rushing around

Ecclesiastes 1:1–11

The author(s) of this book put their reflections on life on the lips of one they call *qohelet*, which NRSV and NIV translate 'Teacher'. The word comes from *qahal*, an assembly or congregation. The word Ecclesiastes ('churchman') itself comes from the Greek word for an assembly, so that gets it right. The theology in this book is the kind that raises more questions than it provides answers, but it is proper 'church' teaching, not some kind of exercise in destructiveness.

I live in a society characterized by a relentless activism. Christians as much as anyone else spend their lives rushing around ceaselessly on the freeway and never stop doing business on their cell-phones. 'What do they gain from it all?' Ecclesiastes asks. Relentlessly they pursue new experiences—new music, new films, new fashions, new holiday destinations. 'The eye is not satisfied with seeing, or the ear filled with hearing,' Ecclesiastes observes. If in due course they collapse in front of the television, the adverts inexorably promise them something new—a new car, a new hamburger, a new computer, an 'all-new episode' of the series that follows. But 'there is nothing new under the sun,' Ecclesiastes comments. Their society through no fault of its own has no past, though it longs for one, and it has no way of knowing what it might look like in the future. 'The people of long ago are not remembered, nor will there be any remembrance of things to come,' Ecclesiastes reflects.

Southern California is the society where Western civilization is tested to destruction, so the rest of the West had better pay attention to how the experiment is going. The West in general lives by the myth of progress. Because technology advances, therefore humanity has progressed. Now I am grateful for the invention of the flush toilet and mains sewage, but it is hard for us to acknowledge that in most areas that matter, humanity has made no progress over the millennia. Ecclesiastes offers to deliver us from our self-deception.

2 The futility of research and self-indulgence

Ecclesiastes 1:12—2:11

The person behind this book is not only a 'churchman' but a son of David and king in Jerusalem. Israel of course had only one person who was traditionally thought of as its great philosopher-king, David's immediate successor, Solomon. His reputation makes him the ideal person to imagine undertaking the investigation that concerns this book. He was the original Southern Californian. He tried everything. He can testify from experience concerning matters that ordinary people can only speculate about. In addition, he had the reputation as the great philosopher. He thought as well as acted. That, too, should enable him to reflect on human experience in an instructive way.

1:12–18 constitutes an introduction to his testimony, summarizing the results of his great experiment. He confirms the claim of 1:2–11, and specifically confirms that our vast human activism cannot achieve things that matter or put right the real problems of the world (1:15). The country that can put a man on the moon cannot solve the problems of poverty, prejudice and inequality in its back yard. The society that puts huge emphasis on research into psychological and social problems cannot enable people to find happiness. The logical result is to be quite disillusioned with the notion of research.

2:1–11 then reports on Solomon's experiment with pleasure in particular. Now if there is a society that has tested pleasure to destruction, it is also the land of Los Angeles, Hollywood and Disneyland. It drinks fine Californian wines and watches countless comedy programmes on television and in the cinema. It is one of the music capitals of the world and one of the sex capitals of the world. It has built fine houses and museums, planted thousands of fruit trees, and constructed monumental irrigation systems. It attracts cheap labour from countries around the world. It comprises half of a state that has an economy greater than that of most of the actual countries in the world. And it is a deeply and widely unhappy society, which proves the truth of the testimony of Solomon without acknowledging the fact to itself.

3 So what shall we do?

Ecclesiastes 2:12–26

Solomon's great experiment does not make him conclude that research, work and relaxation are pointless. They are indeed *absolutely* pointless, but they are nevertheless *relatively* worthwhile. They cannot provide ultimate answers or fulfilment, but they can provide something.

One of the foundations of modernity was the attempt to discover ultimate answers by starting from scratch rather than from supposed 'divine revelation'. Descartes thus began from 'I think, therefore I am'. But the subsequent history of thought has established that philosophy cannot generate answers to ultimate questions. In that sense, wisdom is useless. But wisdom still excels folly as light excels darkness (v. 13). It is *absolutely* useless but *relatively* useful.

One way we seek to find meaning is through work, but our work is also *ultimately* meaningless. Who knows how our successors will carry it on, whether they will ignore it or undo it or prove it wrong? Second-hand bookshops and university library stacks are full of the dusty, now-unread writings of 19th-century biblical scholars, and the works upon which I labour will soon join them. But our work is *relatively* useful. Perhaps my writing these notes may help someone see how Ecclesiastes impacts on their life. That is not nothing.

So in a moment I can break for lunch and rejoice in what I have done this morning (v. 24a). It is a gift of God that I can do that (v. 24b), and this is perhaps one reason why I can rejoice in it. We cannot start from ourselves and reach the conviction that God is there. But if we start from the conviction that God is there, that changes the way we look at our lives and the little things that give meaning to them. And the conviction that God is there and is the source of life's little pleasures is as reasonable a conviction as Descartes's 'I think'. God has not given us the answers to the big questions, but God has not given us nothing.

Straight after that little encouragement, however, Solomon pulls it back. Even our capacity for those little enjoyments is qualified by an awareness that there is a randomness about who receives them (v. 26). Ecclesiastes will not let us turn little answers into the big answer.

4 For everything there is a time

Ecclesiastes 3:1–15

The book abandons Solomon's imagined testimony and moves in a new direction. Different experiences and activities all have their time. The passage speaks of very different kinds of experiences and activities. On one hand, birth and death are events we have no control over. They happen to us; we do not make them happen. The first expression literally means 'a time for giving birth' (AV margin), which suggests a more solemn contrast. Weeping and laughing, mourning and dancing are also experiences built into life. We have no control over the events that provoke them.

In contrast, human discernment and decision-making are involved in planting and uprooting, in demolishing and building, in throwing away or collecting stones (which might be connected with building, but the expressions are a puzzle). The same is true of embracing and refraining from embracing, gestures that suggest entering into friendship and making commitments. It is true of seeking and giving up for lost, keeping and throwing away. It is true of tearing your garments in mourning and repairing them to begin normal life again, and it is true of silence and speaking. It is true of love and hate—in other words, of war and peacemaking. This last pair may also help us to understand the statement that there is a time to kill (the word means 'slay') as well as a time to heal. If 'a time for birthing' means 'a time for being born', perhaps this denotes 'a time for being slain and a time for being healed'.

There are thus uncertainties about the details of this poem, but what about the whole? When the Byrds made it a top ten hit in the 1960s, the idea that there was an appropriate or necessary time for life's activities and experiences presumably came across as a comfort. Ecclesiastes' subsequent comments about times in verse 9–15 fit with that, though they qualify it in a way consistent with 'Solomon's' testimony. Yes, all these human experiences have their time. But what is the framework in which they all fit? God has not told us. It is a clearly postmodern point in a quintessentially postmodern book. We cannot know the nature of the big picture into which everything fits. But perceiving the nature of the little pictures that make up life is not to be despised.

5 In the place of justice, there is wickedness

Ecclesiastes 3:16—4:3

Like the Torah, the Wisdom books interweave theology and ethics. If Ecclesiastes is going to agonize about existential questions, then, they will include ethical ones. Why is there so much injustice in the world? Ecclesiastes was as familiar as we are with a world in which people like him and us are able to control the rules by which society and economics and politics and the law work. Without doing anything illegal, the rich get richer and the poor get poorer. The rich own their land (or their home), eat well, and provide for retirement. The poor do not. In the community of faith (Israel or the Church) there ought to be 'justice and righteousness'. We could paraphrase these as 'power and authority exercised in a way that reflects the rights of people who are bound up together by mutual commitment, like people in a family'. Instead there is 'wickedness, wickedness'. We could paraphrase that as behaviour that ignores the way we are bound together. So what attitude do we take to that?

Suppose we look forward to a day when God will judge everyone (3:17). While there have been occasions when God has intervened in Israel's life in this way, there have been long periods when God has not, and the intervention that may come one day is little use for people who are dying today. If we affirm the conviction that God will undertake a great judgment at the End, there is no empirical evidence for that, and no teaching in Israel's tradition about this either. Ecclesiastes likes being empirical, starting from what we can know. What we know is that everyone dies, human beings as well as animals. What happens afterwards is speculation (3:18–21).

While he then comes back to his regular practical solution, that we should enjoy what we do have (3:22), he follows that with a more gloomy alternative perspective. Our human inhumanity to one another is indeed overwhelming. People who have not been born and have therefore not yet witnessed it are more fortunate than those who have (4:1–3).

6 The advantages of companionship; the perils of religion

Ecclesiastes 4:4—5:7

The attempt to achieve is an inherently lone venture. We are seeking to make our mark, to do better than the next man. I use the gender-specific language advisedly, because in our culture this has usually been a male affair. The same seems to have been true of Ecclesiastes' culture. Ecclesiastes' exhortation is one that in our culture women have more often instinctively lived by, though they have now been able to join the rat race. The book urges that collaborative work is better than individual work. Admittedly its argument is very down-to-earth in the advantages it sees in two people working together (4:10–12a). Three people working together is even better (4:12b).

Ecclesiastes is also down-to-earth in the insight he offers on religion. His first warning corresponds to one that recurs in the prophets. A well-to-do person, at least, is able to do just the right thing by way of sacrifices, but this may not be accompanied by the kind of life that God approves outside the temple. It is wiser to listen to what prophets, priests, and philosopher/ethicists have to say (5:1). The Torah itself was never interested in sacrifice unaccompanied by right living.

Second, the Psalter is full of praises to sing and protests to utter, some going on at great length. Ecclesiastes believes we need to set the awareness of God's awesomeness alongside the awareness of God's approachability (5:2–3). We might compare the stress on reverence and awe in Hebrews 12 with the stress on childlike freedom in Romans 8.

Third, both the Torah and the Psalms also assume that people often make promises to God, but Ecclesiastes wants people to think before they pledge. Don't make a promise you are not prepared to fulfil (5:4–6). This might be a special danger at a moment of great enthusiasm in worship, or of great personal need.

Fourth, the development of apocalypses such as Daniel reflects the way God can guide through dreams. Ecclesiastes joins with a prophet such as Jeremiah who emphasizes the way in which dreams that allegedly come from God may actually come from people's own imaginations (5:7). How the sentence works is obscure, but the punch line is clear: 'have reverence for

God'. Translations tend to render this phrase 'fear God', but Ecclesiastes no more wants people to be afraid of God than other Old or New Testament writers do.

Guidelines

What is the significance of this extraordinary book? Here are some possibilities to consider:

- Is it a statement of the darkness into which the gospel came? It has been used in evangelistic Bible studies to help people face the reality of life without Christ.
- Is it an essentially positive book—one that first portrays the nature of the darkness, and then shines out with light?
- Is it a book that gives believers permission to face hard questions? We do not have to avoid these, even if we cannot always answer them very well.
- Is it a book that actually urges believers to face hard questions, rather than pretending that we have all the answers?
- Is it a book that simply acknowledges the contradictoriness of life and faith, and leaves us with it?

Which makes sense of your own reading of the book and of you yourself, in the light of what it is and what you are?

1 The best things in life are free?

Ecclesiastes 5:8—6:9

One of Ecclesiastes' recurrent themes is money. It acknowledges that money is really important, but urges that it is less important than people think.

- It is strangely deceptive, or strangely unfulfilling (5:10). A current television advert acknowledges that the most precious things in life are priceless, but for all the rest we have a certain credit card. We decline to acknowledge that more money and things will do us no good (cf. 6:7–9). And as a result, we are inhibited from enabling some poor people (for whom a little more could make a huge difference) to have that little more.

- Increased wealth never seems to go as far as you think it will (5:11). The cost of acquiring it has to be offset against the gain from it.
- Increased wealth brings anxiety with it. An ordinary working man may not have much, but he has enough, and he does not have to worry about how the stock market is faring (5:12).
- This wealth is always precarious. You can never be sure you will make the right decision about when to buy and when to sell (5:13–14a). You can make a bad decision and end up with nothing, which is hard in itself, but even harder when you put so much effort into making your money in the first place instead of (say) lying on the beach (5:14b–16).
- Or your affairs may collapse through no fault of your own, or death may deprive you of the chance to enjoy them (6:1–6). Then your anger and frustration can make you much more unhappy than the person who never had what you lost (5:17).

We have to sit loose to money, and a starting point is acknowledging what Ecclesiastes says. The sensible thing is to enjoy the good things of life that God gives, without pretending that they can provide ultimate satisfaction or meaning. Once more, they are not everything, but they are not nothing (5:18–20).

2 Facing human limitations

Ecclesiastes 7:1–7, 23–29

Call no one happy till they are dead, said the Athenian statesman and philosopher, Solon. Only then can you make a definitive judgment. Death is a good thing, then, because it makes a definitive judgment possible (7:1). The comment reminds us how temporary our reputations can be, and how provisional our judgments must be.

We are going to die. It is a fact that we work hard to avoid. Ecclesiastes believes that it has decisive importance for the life we live before death. Keeping aware of where we are bound helps us make happier decisions now. Only a fool forgets that (7:2–4). It is but one facet of the fool's unreliability (7:5–7).

Again Ecclesiastes reminds us that his conclusions have

limited significance (7:23–25). Here he seems to be reverting to giving 'Solomon's' testimony about what he has discovered. This is supported by the introduction of another reference to the 'Teacher' in verse 27, the first since 1:12. That may point to part of the explanation for what follows.

Verses 26–29 seem extraordinarily misogynistic, and puzzlingly so. How could their author go on to write 9:9? Indeed, verse 29 (which suggests that all human beings fail) looks in tension with verse 28 (which suggests an exception to that rule). Further, 'man' in verse 28 (*adam*) is actually the word for a human being, the word that recurs in verse 29. This underlines the problem.

Three possibilities may help us with the text. First, if 'Solomon' speaks again, the thousand women are the ones mentioned in 1 Kings 11:3, whom he indeed allowed to lead him astray. The warning is then couched as a warning about women, but ironically so, because it is as much a warning to men about themselves. Second, an implication would be that if this is one man's warning testimony about the mess one can get into with women (a warning about our capacities as men!), then it invites a responsive formulation in which women reflect on the way men can be 'bitter as death'. Third, Roland Murphy among other commentators neatly undoes the problem by changing the punctuation of verse 28: 'What my mind has sought repeatedly, but I have not found, is that 'one human being among a thousand I found, but a woman among all these I have not found'. This statement is one Ecclesiastes goes on to disagree with. Men are not even one-tenth of a per cent better than women. All have perverted their way. It is an even gloomier conclusion, worthy of Ecclesiastes.

3 Facing the facts about death

Ecclesiastes 9:1–12

Here are the facts, then. First, death comes to everyone (9:1–3, 11–12). God is the one who gives life and the one who eventually takes it back, but we can see no rationale about how God does that. The righteous and wicked, the clean and polluted, the good and evil, the religious and the irreligious, the wise and the mad, the people who take oaths and the people who refrain from this: they all die. Belonging to the first group ought to make some difference: maybe you should live longer. But both groups are in God's hand, and how and when you die seems to be a matter of whim.

Second, death means your human experience is all over (9:4–6, 10b). You have no hope. While you are alive, you may still have prospects. When you are dead, you have none. Nothing will ever again happen to you. Death means no knowing, no reward, no being remembered, no loving, no hating, no jealousy, no acting, no thinking.

Ecclesiastes presupposes some practical facts about death that are common to Old Testament thinking as a whole. They overlap with death as we experience it, though not as we always think about it. Old Testament faith assumes that what happens to the body is a guide to what happens to the person. This is a natural assumption if you believe that the body is a true expression of the person, but the hold of Greek thinking on Christian faith often makes us assume that the body does not really matter.

When a person dies, the life visibly disappears from them. They cannot move, act, laugh, cry, or worship. If the body cannot do these things, it is hardly conceivable that the person (the 'soul') can do so. Being human is too bodily for that. We await the resurrection of our bodies so we can do these things again. But Ecclesiastes had no basis for believing in such resurrection, and insists on being rigorously empirical and not consoling us with pie in the sky when you die.

It is precisely against the background of the fact of death that Ecclesiastes invites his audience to affirm life (9:7–10a). The fact that it is all we have is reason for enjoying it, not for devaluing it.

4 Attitudes to the king

Ecclesiastes 9:13—10:20

In Egypt, teaching of the kind that we have in the Old Testament Wisdom books was collected to form a resource for the education of people who would work in the civil service. Both Proverbs and Ecclesiastes include material on how to relate to the king, and this might form a natural part of wisdom for someone involved with the royal court. Ecclesiastes' material on the subject reflects his characteristic hard-nosed stance.

First, an ordinary person with insight may fulfil a role that is actually more important than the king's, but ordinary people are unlikely to be remembered for that (9:13–18). One senses that Ecclesiastes would rather be the ordinary person with insight than the person who merely has position and power. It is another sign that Ecclesiastes is hardly to be identified with Solomon in real life.

Second, you need to be able to keep cool if you work at court (10:4). As long as the king stops short of 'off with his head', keeping cool will probably be your salvation.

Third, on the other hand Ecclesiastes is a political and social conservative and believes in the proper order of things (10:5–7). There are people who belong to the ruling class and people who belong to the ruled, and both should stay in their place. Otherwise chaos rules (cf. 10:16–17).

Fourth, you need discretion if you are to survive (10:20). It is amazing how rulers sometimes get to know things.

The material on kingship is not very coherent and thus mirrors the nature of Ecclesiastes as a whole. One of the perceptive commentators on the book, Michael V. Fox, has written about *Qohelet and His Contradictions* (Sheffield, 1989). It is one of the glories of Ecclesiastes not to oversimplify things. Both the theoretical questions about life, and the practical ones, are complicated.

5 Remember your Creator in the days of your youth

Read Ecclesiastes 11:7—12:7

The contradictoriness of Ecclesiastes continues in this last section of the concrete teaching in the book. On the one hand, we are to enjoy our lives. As young people we are to rejoice in our youth, as old people we are to rejoice in the number of years we are given, and we are to 'think positive'. Yet we are also to keep in mind that youth yields to old age, life yields to death, the length of life is far exceeded by the time we spend dead, and in old age continuing life can become more a burden than a privilege.

12:1–7 constitutes a profound conclusion to Ecclesiastes' treatment of death, though a puzzling one. The puzzlement and the profundity issue from its combining several pictures, which interweave literal description and imagery to convey the loss that old age and death involve.

The first image is that of fading light and a gathering storm (12:2). The picture of old age begins with an equivalent to our talk of the autumn of our lives. The image reverses the process in Genesis 1 whereby God brings light into being and sets sun, moon and stars in the sky. In old age, a person may have more and more difficulty seeing the light, and at death these lights go out for the individual.

The second image is a great house gradually falling into disrepair and disuse (12:3-4). Its staff and its inhabitants are getting older and incapable. The house has lost its place as a centre of life and activity in the community. The silence of death has descended upon it.

Third, the passage pictures an old man losing his faculties. Initially it speaks more literally (12:5a), though it complicates this by describing his deterioration by means of a number of figures (12:5b). One way or another the passage describes the increasing weakness of old age.

Finally the passage portrays the arrival of death itself (12:6-7). It does this first in figures and then in theological language that again sees death as a reversing of God's acts of creation, when God shaped the first man's body from dirt and breathed life into it. The life-breath disappears and the body dissolves.

Ecclesiastes is not wrong. There may be more to be said about what happens after we die, but that can only be said after we have accepted the facts that Ecclesiastes urges.

6 The value of a goad

Ecclesiastes 12:8-14

The book closes where it began, only more so. 'Vanity of vanities', it repeats from 1:2. The expression forms a bracket round its teaching. 'Vanity' (hebel) is one of Ecclesiastes' favourite words. He is responsible for half its appearances in the Old Testament. Literally it means a breath or a breeze, but it is usually used figuratively to denote something that has no substance. It is often applied to images of gods, which have no substance and are useless and empty. The repetition of the word suggests 'utter emptiness', 'utter futility'. The conviction from which the book starts is that life goes nowhere and history manifests no progress, and this fact makes human life look quite empty. The conviction with which it closes is that the fact of death carries the same implications.

The last paragraph of the book then closes in the third person, so that 12:9–14 pairs with 1:1. Whoever wrote or compiled the material in 1:2—12:8 with that summarizing bracket around it, the opening and close of the book are someone else's comments. In his study of the way different books of the Old Testament are 'shaped to function' as canon, *An Introduction to the Old Testament as Scripture*, Brevard S. Childs has particular success with Ecclesiastes. He shows how these opening and closing words invite readers into a balanced attitude to this book as these words take it on its journey towards becoming scripture.

On one hand, we have noted that these comments begin by calling the writer 'churchman'. They now repeat the term, and add that what we have been reading is indeed the work of a 'wise man'. This is a theological term in the Old Testament, not a merely academic one. These are words of truth, well-taught (12:10). The summary goes on to a brilliant encapsulation of how this wise man's teachings work. They are like goads (12:11). They hurt you, they make you say 'Ouch', but they do that in order to drive you forward. Once the kind of thing that Ecclesiastes says is out there, it cannot be unsaid.

On the other hand, enough is enough (12:12). One Ecclesiastes in the canon is a good idea. A canon full of Ecclesiasteses would not be. The reader needs to keep in mind the basic convictions of wisdom and to set Ecclesiastes in its context (12:13). The fact that there is no empirical evidence for some statements of faith does not mean they are not true (12:14).

Guidelines

As I write these notes, my wife is lying on the settee at the other end of the room, to safeguard against her getting pressure sores. She has multiple sclerosis. Twenty years ago, she worked as a psychiatrist. Just last week we had a Christmas card from one of her psychotherapy patients, who remembers the sessions she had with Ann and looks back on them as a decisive shaping influence on her life. Today Ann cannot remember what country she lives in, nor what day it is, nor what are the names of the two carers who have shared in looking after her for over two years, nor what is the name of the grandson who brought her such joy when he was here a few weeks ago. She is virtually unable to swallow (she eats via a feeding tube) or to speak. She is watching the television news, though I am not sure how much she takes in. On that news we have been hearing of the terrible cost of the Russian invasion of Chechnya, of the suffering of the local people and of the Russian bodies surrounding their tanks. The pictures were too grim to show us. In a moment I will take her out for a walk in her wheelchair in the warm January sun, and we will have an ice-cream, and if we are lucky she will be able to eat a little of it, and as I push her back up the hill to our apartment I will sing silly songs and pretend I am not going to make it to the top, and she will laugh. It is not enough, but it is not nothing, and it is certainly not to be despised. It is a gift from God. That is what Ecclesiastes says. It is also a wonderful gift from God that this book should be in the canon of scripture. I cannot imagine how it got through some community screening procedure. Actually I can. I do not think they were fooled by the reference to Solomon. I think they were overcome by the truth it speaks.

FOR FURTHER READING

Robert Davidson, *Ecclesiastes and Song of Solomon*, St Andrew Press, 1986

Wesley J. Fuerst, *The Five Scrolls*, Cambridge, 1975

Roland Murphy, *Ecclesiastes*, Word Books, 1992

R. N. Whybray, *Ecclesiastes*, Sheffield, 1989

DAY BY DAY
WITH GOD

Bible Readings for Women

Day by Day with God (published jointly with Christina Press) is written especially by women for women, with a regular team of contributors. Each four-monthly issue offers daily Bible readings, with key verses printed out, helpful comment and a prayer for the day ahead. Our readings in this sampler come from Elaine Pountney, a conference and retreat speaker currently working as a management consultant.

Mark 11:9–10 (NIV)

Backing a winner

'Hosanna! Blessed is he who comes in the name of the Lord! ...
Hosanna in the highest!'

The street was noisy, messy with cloaks and palm branches, and chaotic in its exuberant response to Jesus. This king came riding on the colt of a donkey, symbolic of a king arriving in peace. The people welcomed this king with the traditional greeting reserved for pilgrims arriving in Jerusalem to celebrate the Passover: 'Blessed is he who comes in the name of the Lord.'

The air pulsated with hope mixed with pleas for help: 'hosanna, save us now!' But what did the people need saving from—or what did they think they needed rescue from? Maybe from oppressive tax burdens. From foreigners disrespectful of their faith, traditions and worship. But did they have any idea that they might need rescuing from themselves?

The people seemed convinced they were backing a winner, a king who would rescue them and painlessly put right all that oppressed them. They were filled with hope, optimistic that they would be rescued from the mundane merry-go-round of everyday weariness. Or more seriously from cruelty and injustice.

How often I have pleaded for rescue ('Hosanna me, Jesus!') and daydreamed that Jesus would dramatically take the hard bits of life away—this cancer, my son's arthritis, my barrenness. That he would whisk away the people that make my life so difficult—those relationships that silence and shame me. I have often cried out, 'A miracle, Jesus—just this one miracle.' Surprisingly, or maybe not, that is not his style.

Rather, just as he did in Jerusalem so many years ago, Jesus comes riding on a donkey, bringing peace into my life, not magical escape —bringing himself into my life.

I find that profoundly comforting.

Jesus, thank you for the comfort and quietness of your presence. In that quiet comfort, hosanna us—save us. Save us from ourselves.

EP

Scary student and business executive

'My house will be called a house of prayer for all nations.'
But you have made it a den of robbers.

The following day, after entering Jerusalem in peace, Jesus unleashes his fury in the temple area. Fury at corrupt money-changers ripping off pilgrims of prayer. Fury at extortion by the high priest's henchmen selling sacrificial animals at inflated prices.

Tables flying, coins clinking, merchants scrambling, cattle and sheep stampeding out, doves flapping and squawking wildly in the confusion. Whip in hand, Jesus restores the temple as a house of prayer for all nations—a place of petition and praise.

Do you ever wonder what Jesus' face must have looked like in this passionate cleansing of his Father's house of prayer? Or what his voice sounded like rising above the pandemonium, shouting: 'My house will be called a house of prayer for all nations. But you have made it a den of robbers'?

It makes me wonder, what have we made God's house into in our own time?

Near the end of a conversation I had today with a very successful young business executive, he told me that he prayed every night before he went to bed. I nearly fell off my chair! He said he felt like his soul was crying out from inside of him, calling for help. Here is a young man, searching for God; and where are our houses of prayer for him—an unchurched seeker of God?

Two days ago I had a conversation with a young university student—body piercing extraordinaire—wearing a chain-link necklace with a heavy-duty lock. Pretty scary looking—and a student of genuine Christian faith. Not surprisingly, he was finding it difficult to find a church to fit into. Where is God's house of prayer for the young of our nation? For those of genuine faith seeking a place of prayer?

These conversations have made me stop and ask what Jesus would see if he walked into our churches today? A house of prayer or a den of robbers?

EP

Entrusted with the house of prayer

Be on guard! Be alert! ... You do not know when the owner of the house will come back... do not let him find you sleeping.

It was all carefully planned. Party time Saturday night. Clean up before Mum and Dad return. Simple... well, not exactly. Our daughters hadn't counted on the unexpected guests turning up—drunk and disorderly! They hadn't counted on the overall mess, or the broken table, or the ripped-out light fixture. They hadn't counted on not being able to control the circumstances.

When we walked into our house on return from a week's retreat, something felt wrong. We couldn't put our finger on it right away but we soon saw the remnants of the party from the night before. We had trusted our daughters—and entrusted them—with our home, theirs and ours. They were just not ready for our return and reunion.

On Sunday, we read how Jesus entered Jerusalem as a king of peace. On Monday, we read how this king of peace re-established a place of prayer for all nations in Jerusalem. Today we read serious warnings by Jesus, calling his followers to be on guard—to be alert!

Alert for what? Alert for King Jesus to return to earth, and to be ready to meet him at that time. Jesus said there would be difficult, even terrible times before his return: earthquakes and famines, wars and rumours of wars, persecution of believers, false teaching and false teachers. But even through these difficult times, we are to be on guard and not asleep. We are to be ready for our king's return.

And just how will we be ready? By making every day of our lives fit for our king's return. By keeping his house a house of prayer rather than a house out of control. By completing the work he gives us each day—the work of belief and of love, the work of building up the family of God and of prayer.

Our biggest danger is falling asleep on the job!

EP

Mark 14:3–9 (NIV)

The goodness of extravagance

While he was in Bethany… a woman came with an alabaster jar of very expensive perfume, made of pure nard. She broke the jar and poured the perfume on his head.

The scene: a comfortable home in the suburb of Bethany. The time: the week of preparation before the major religious and cultural celebration of the year. The players: Jesus, good friends of Jesus, disciples of Jesus.

The scene opens with the potent aroma of an expensive, exotic perfume filling the room. A woman has broken an alabaster jar of nard and poured it on the head of Jesus, the religious teacher who is reclining at the table. He simply receives this extravagant and unusual gift from the woman.

Some of the guests in the house are expressing indignation. 'What a waste! She just dumped a year's worth of wages on Jesus' head. And he does nothing! It could have been sold and the money given to the poor.'

Well, they've got a point, haven't they… or have they? *What is the point?* The point is that Jesus loves our spontaneous gifts of love and affection, just as he loves to give spontaneous gifts of love and affection. Jesus' defence of the woman's gift of anointing is swift and clear: 'Leave her alone. You'll always have the poor with you. She has done a beautiful thing to me. What she has done will always be told with the gospel.'

How extraordinary! For Jesus this is a beautiful thing and for those around it is a waste. Jesus so graciously receives this extravagant gift of love and generosity from the woman as a gift of preparation for his death—one of the last acts of kindness before his death. And in return, Jesus gives her a beautiful gift of affirmation and acknowledgment. I want to be like that!

Oh God, let my heart be free and spontaneous in extravagant and extraordinary acts of love and blessing. Guard me from 'righteous' indignation.

EP

Mark 14:32–42 (NIV)

The body is weak

Then he returned to his disciples and found them sleeping…
'Could you not keep watch for one hour? Watch and pray so that
you will not fall into temptation. The spirit is willing, but the
body is weak.'

At the beginning of Lent I decided that I wanted to use this time to
discipline myself and remove some of the interminable busyness of
my life. I had heard a brilliant talk challenging us to pick something
up for Lent rather than the usual giving something up for Lent.

Yes, I thought. That was a great idea. I thought that for each day
in Lent I would be quiet, read the Bible and pray for one hour. Piece
of cake, I thought. Well, I expect you know what happened. Two
days into Lent, the busyness of my life completely obliterated any
thoughts of an hour of quiet—let alone space.

It wasn't that I didn't want to be quiet and meditate each day—
I was willing. But somehow all my busyness and all the distractions
of my life choked my intentions. It makes me think of so many diets
and exercise disciplines I've tried! But that's another story.

The disciples were willing—Jesus knew that. He also knew that
their bodies were weak. They were tired and weary. Tragically, they
simply didn't understand what this was all about until it was too late
to support and care for Jesus and themselves. How often have I
missed such opportunities?

Jesus asked his disciples three times to watch and pray with
him. Just the day before, Jesus had talked with them about the
importance of staying alert so they wouldn't be found sleeping. And
here they are in the garden snoring up a storm. They missed being
with Jesus in his moment of need.

That night, when Jesus was overwhelmed to the point of death
(v. 34), in deep anguish over his impending death, they snored on.

Us too?

EP

Mark 15:21–41 (NIV)

Bridging the gap

'My God, my God, why have you forsaken me?' … With a loud cry, Jesus breathed his last.

Jesus dying on a cross. *Can this really be the Son of God—the king who will save us?* Soldiers gambling for Jesus' robe as he hung in pain. *Caught in the moment, they miss the love of God.* The morbid curiosity of a man who wanted to see if Elijah would rescue Jesus from the cross. *Would he have believed if Elijah had?* A tough, hardened Roman soldier who hears Jesus' cry and utters, 'Surely this man was the Son of God!' *Was that belief or just observation?* Two thieves dying similar deaths with Jesus: one cynical, one believing. *Where would they be tomorrow morning?*

Could it be that these facets of human nature were part of the completion of God's plan of rescue for men and women just like them? Could it be that God would die alone in the midst of callous human nature, their eyes glued to his hanging body, waiting to see if he would jump down from the cross? Could Jesus do no more than look helpless and weak in comparison to the hardness of humanity around him?

Alongside stood the ever faithful women, still caring for Jesus in his suffering and death—just by being there. *Would they still have faith tomorrow?* Disciples peered from a distance, trying to make sense of their beloved teacher, so helpless, jeered and spat upon. *Was his teaching powerless too?* Men once blind, now miraculously healed, watched him die a gruesome death. *Would their eyes hold on to the light?* Lepers once barred from public spectacles pushed their way in to behold their miracle worker run out of miracles for himself. *What miracle will keep them in the Kingdom now?*

Unable to bear more, Jesus finally cries out: 'My God, my God, why have you forsaken me?' (v. 34). Jesus takes upon himself all human sin. The earth trembles and convulses as the Son of God gasps in death.

'With a loud cry, Jesus breathed his last' (v. 37). It is finished. Jesus dies.

EP

41

Mark 15:42–47 (NIV)

Lovingly wrapped in secrecy

So Joseph bought some linen cloth, took down the body, wrapped it in the linen, and placed it in a tomb cut out of rock.

The Son of God was dead, his work finished and complete. It was about three o'clock in the afternoon and evening was rapidly approaching. The body of Jesus would be left hanging until after the sabbath if not taken down before sunset. Joseph acted quickly to get permission from Pilate to remove Jesus' body. Although surprised at the quickness of Jesus' death, Pilate gave permission.

Joseph is a curious character in the death of Jesus. He was a prominent member of the Council—or the Sanhedrin. He was very probably at the trial of Jesus the night before when Jesus was judged and condemned. And, according to John, he was a secret disciple of Jesus (19:38–42).

Joseph is accompanied by another curious character—Nicodemus. Nicodemus, who came to Jesus at night for a conversation (John 3). Nicodemus, who was confused about having to be born again. What a curious pair.

These two once-secret disciples take Jesus' body down from the cross and prepare it for the grave. They caringly wrap the body in strips of linen and a mixture of myrrh and aloes, then lay Jesus in a new tomb. All the while the women watch to see where the body will be laid.

Jesus started his earthly life wrapped lovingly in strips of cloth by his mother and being gently laid to rest in a manger. When he was a child, Magi from the east brought the baby Jesus gifts, including myrrh. Now, in his death, at the end of his earthly life, he is wrapped lovingly in strips of cloth and myrrh by two secret but faithful disciples and is gently laid to rest by two men who loved him, in a tomb carved in stone.

And when Jesus' body is laid to rest on that eve of Passover, Joseph of Arimathea, Nicodemus and the women return to their homes to rest on the sabbath.

EP

Mark 16:1–8 (NIV)

He is risen! He is not here

'Don't be alarmed... He has risen! He is not here. See the place where they laid him...' Trembling and bewildered, the women went out and fled from the tomb. They said nothing to anyone, because they were afraid.

Finally the sabbath is over. Dawn is just beginning in the east. And the women bustle about with their spices and supplies to anoint and preserve Jesus' body. Wrapped in their own feelings of grief, of disbelief, and of loss, these faithful women leave to perform their last act of caring for Jesus.

And suddenly, an obvious question: the stone. Who will roll the stone away from the entrance of the tomb? And yet they keep on walking, wondering about the stone and how they will move it. When they arrive, the stone has already been rolled away. What a relief! They can complete the final preparations of Jesus' body—a final act of love to bring closure to Jesus' death. So they enter the tomb looking for Jesus' body. Instead they find an angel, saying, 'Jesus has risen!'

They are alarmed and terrified. Even after the angel tries to calm their alarm, they tremble in bewilderment. Risen? What on earth does 'risen' mean? Has he been stolen? Is this a political thing? Have we simply come too late? But 'risen'—what is that? They leave the tomb and flee!

So would I! I've never met an angel or a resurrected person. But I have often gone looking for Jesus only to discover he's not where I expect him to be. And he doesn't look like I expect him to look! Just like the women, I too am often bewildered, not knowing where to find him or what to do with his angels.

Sometimes I arrive to discover that he's just left. Sometimes I just don't get what's going on. I think the women just didn't know what to make of this—they didn't know what was going on.

So what was going on? Jesus is going on—he's alive!

Alleluia! He is risen. He is risen indeed.

EP

Rolling away the stone of grief

'Woman,' he said, 'why are you crying? Who is it you are looking for?'

The pain and the loss at his death were overwhelming. Jesus, this teacher, who knew her so well and still loved her, had given her dignity and respect. He had called seven demons out of her and still he let her journey with him and with his disciples. When others had discounted and disrespected her, Jesus honoured her.

In the imagination of memory, she can remember the look of love in his face, his tenderness with her brokenness, his gentleness.

Now he was dead.

All she wanted to do was to weep and mourn his death and say goodbye to him—but his body was gone. There would be no last farewell. Here in the garden, she felt as empty as the tomb. Her grief felt like a huge stone, sunk deep within her, lodged permanently in place within her.

And then she heard something. Her name—*her own name!* And that voice. She knew that voice. No, it couldn't be! Whirling around, not daring to believe, her tears gave way to sight and she saw him. He was alive! He was there in front of her. She flung her arms around him and cried out, '*Rabboni!*' (Teacher).

The stone was dislodged and rolled away. Her grief turned to joy and her mourning to amazement. Jesus immediately unwrapped her arms from around him and gave her a mission: 'Go and tell.' And that's exactly what she did. She went and found the disciples and told them what had happened: 'I have seen the Lord!'

We have so many stones lodged in place deep within us from losses and grief in our lives. And like Mary we continue to wait outside these tombs of life. Perhaps it's time to turn from these tombs and see Jesus.

Jesus, come and find us in the graveyards of our life and gently call us by name. Come and find us.

EP

Luke 24:13–35 (NIV)

Rolling away the stone of blindness

Then their eyes were opened and they recognized him, and he disappeared from their sight. They asked each other, 'Were not our hearts burning within us while he talked with us on the road and opened the scriptures to us?'

Deep in conversation, trying to make sense of the events of the last week, two disciples walk along a road together. Jesus surreptitiously slides into place alongside them and, unrecognized, he joins their discussion and their journey.

These disciples are amazed that this newcomer to their conversation seems ignorant of the facts of the last week. Didn't he know about this Jesus? So they tell the story of Jesus. During the conversation Jesus begins to challenge and push their thinking while opening the scriptures where they were blind in their understanding.

At the end of their journey they urge Jesus to stay the evening with them. During dinner Jesus takes bread, breaks it and gives thanks. Suddenly their blindness turns to understanding and they *know*: it is Jesus. He *is* risen! He *is* present!

That's just the way it happens, isn't it? We get so busy trying to figure things out and trying to make sense of things that we are often blind to the fact that Jesus is right in the middle of our figuring out. And then suddenly, like a match being struck in a dark room, our hearts burn within us and we see. Only problem is, Jesus seems to have gone on. And we find ourselves running—somewhere, to someone—trying to find someone to share our excitement with: 'It is true! The Lord is alive and is with us.'

How often we miss the smile of Jesus on the train, or a kindness in the supermarket, a thoughtfulness in our office, or someone asking us how we are. And we simply miss Jesus because we are so wrapped up in our own thoughts.

Jesus, roll the stone of our blindness away that we might see you in new ways, in new places, in new people today.

EP

John 20:19–23 (NIV)

Rolling away the stone of fear

On the evening of that first day of the week, when the disciples were together, with the doors locked for fear of the Jews, Jesus came and stood among them and said, 'Peace be with you!'

They had talked with Mary, who had seen Jesus, and Peter and John had run and discovered the empty tomb. So the disciples called an executive meeting—to talk, strategize, and make sense of what all this meant—in secret, behind locked doors. They were frightened for their own lives, terrified that they too would be killed because of their association with Jesus.

Suddenly, without warning, Jesus stands among the huddled disciples and speaks, 'Peace be with you!' With those words come memories of crashing waves calmed, of howling winds silenced, of clutching hands cramped on the boat gunnels in a storm, of fishermen fearing for their lives. Jesus' words from that storm come back: 'Why are you so afraid? Do you still have no faith?' (Mark 4:40).

Jesus understood their fear of death—he had just come from there. So he speaks peace to them huddled in fear behind locked doors, struggling with questions of faith. Then Jesus shows the disciples his hands and side—eternal wounds that prove he understands their fears.

Finally, they get it! It all begins to make sense.

But Jesus doesn't stop there. He gives them a mission: 'As the Father has sent me, I am sending you. Be my hands, be my feet, be my words, be my heart in the world as I was for our Father in heaven.'

My heart misses a beat reading Jesus' mission for his disciples. Doesn't Jesus get it? He has just been killed for being holy hands and feet—and he has the scars to prove it! To be sent as he was sent was a high-risk proposition. No wonder disciples need the gift of peace! The stone of fear begins to move.

And then another gift: 'Receive the Holy Spirit.' They are not alone. Nor will they ever be alone. The Spirit will always be with them.

EP

John 20:24–29 (NIV)

Rolling away the stone of doubt

'Unless I see the nail marks in his hands and put my finger where the nails were, and put my hand into his side, I will not believe it.'

Where was Thomas the night before, when Jesus showed up in the disciples' meeting? Was he out walking alone on the hills? Struggling with the faith he had put in Jesus—his uncompromising honesty with himself about what he believed?

Perhaps Thomas' way of struggling through his grief and his confusion was by being alone. His world was suddenly more chaotic than it had ever been and that probably didn't sit easily on his shoulders. And so he missed the disciples' meeting and Jesus' blessing of peace. He also missed when Jesus showed the other disciples the wounds in his hands and his side.

When Thomas did finally meet with the disciples they must have bubbled out their encounter with Jesus. But Thomas cannot pretend to believe when he doesn't. How can he? It doesn't make any sense. He cannot find a parking space for resurrection in his head. He has to be sure on this one. And at this moment, he wasn't.

There are so many things that I wrestle with in my head that just don't seem to find a parking space there—like resurrection; or believing that God really will take care of me, I don't have to do it all by myself; or believing that God really does love me.

But later, at another meeting, still behind locked doors, Thomas is with the disciples. And Jesus shows up again: 'Come and see, Thomas. Stop doubting and believe.' Thomas' response is instantaneous and clear: 'My Lord and my God!'

Jesus rolled the stone of doubt away. Thomas is a believer.

Thank you, Jesus, for the respectful and loving ways in which you seek us out in our places of doubt. But some of our stones of doubt, Jesus, are very big and very stuck. Dislodge them. Roll them away. Release us into belief.

EP

Rolling away the stone of alienation

'Simon, son of John, do you truly love me more than these? …
Simon, son of John, do you truly love me? … Simon, son of John,
do you love me?'

Late one post-resurrection day, Peter heads off to go fishing—that
was his job, after all—and some of the disciples decide to join him.
After fishing all night without much success they head for shore.
Someone on the shore calls out and suggests they cast the net on
the right side of the boat. They do, and catch 153 fish! John realizes
that the 'someone' on shore is Jesus and tells Peter. And in true,
impulsive Peter-fashion, Peter takes the plunge and swims to shore.
Meanwhile the other disciples bring Peter's boat in and soon enjoy
a breakfast cooked by Jesus.

After breakfast Jesus asks Peter, 'Do you truly love me more than
these?' Three times Jesus asks this question. Peter must have
immediately remembered how he had betrayed Jesus and three
times denied even knowing him. *Doesn't Jesus understand how painful*
this is to Peter? Doesn't he understand the pressure Peter is under? Of
course, Peter is hurt, but three times his response is a simple, 'Yes,
Lord, you know that I love you.' And with that extraordinary
encounter, the broken relationship between Jesus and Peter is
healed.

I always want Jesus simply to throw his arms around Peter and
say, 'There, there, Peter. It's OK.' But Jesus never goes for sticking
plaster, he always goes for major surgery. He knew that Peter needed
deep reconciliation after he had betrayed Jesus—a deep surgical
procedure of character. This was the right time for that painful
surgical cut of correction.

Have you ever experienced Jesus' surgical skill, those deep cuts
for character correction? I have. And I'm grateful that Jesus would
be bothered to care enough to thoughtfully and carefully make the
necessary incisions.

After surgery came a mission: 'If you love me, then take care of
my people—my lambs, my sheep. Feed them. Care for them as I
myself would.' And with that, Jesus rolled away the stone of
alienation.

EP

Rolling away the stone of comparison

When Peter saw [the disciple whom Jesus loved], he asked, 'Lord, what about him?' Jesus answered, 'If I want him to remain alive until I return, what is that to you? You must follow me.'

After Jesus and Peter are reconciled, Jesus talks with Peter about how Peter is going to die. 'When you were younger you dressed yourself and went where you wanted; but when you are old you will stretch out your hands, and someone else will dress you and lead you where you do not want to go.'

These comments by Jesus must have been quite overwhelming for Peter. He had cracked under the pressure of Jesus' trial and crucifixion and now he was being told that he would die a similar death—whew! My mind would race right back into fear and panic and paralysis just at the possibility of suffering such pain.

Peter's way of dealing with Jesus' comment is to compare himself with the disciple John. 'What about him? How is he going to die?' Jesus says, 'What is that to you, Peter? Your task is to follow me.'

I'm just like that at times when I am frightened and want someone else's options. I skip right over my fear and my terror and jump into attack: 'Why do I get all the grunge jobs? Why can't I have John's place?' How easy to think that God is taking more notice of others and even likes them better.

So Jesus refocuses Peter. He reminds Peter that people's journeys are tailor-made. Not comparable, not transferable. One journey; one person.

Gently Jesus invites: 'Peter, you must follow me'—not John! That is our task as well—to follow Jesus wherever he leads us; to keep our eyes on him and the journey that belongs uniquely to us, and not into the tombs and deadness of comparisons and competition.

Jesus, keep rolling away our stone of comparison so that we can follow you into our unique journey.

EP

PBC INTRODUCTION

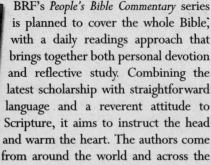

BRF's *People's Bible Commentary* series is planned to cover the whole Bible, with a daily readings approach that brings together both personal devotion and reflective study. Combining the latest scholarship with straightforward language and a reverent attitude to Scripture, it aims to instruct the head and warm the heart. The authors come from around the world and across the Christian traditions, and offer serious yet accessible commentary. The series is an invaluable resource for first-time students of the Bible, for all who read the Bible regularly, for study group leaders, and anyone involved in preaching and teaching Scripture. Volumes are published twice a year, and the series is scheduled for completion in 2005.

The General Editors for the series are the Revd Dr Richard A. Burridge, New Testament scholar and Dean of King's College, London; Dom Henry Wansbrough OSB, Master of St Benet's Hall, Oxford and editor of The New Jerusalem Bible; Canon David Winter, writer, broadcaster and Consulting Editor for BRF's *New Daylight* Bible reading notes.

Our PBC extracts in this sampler are from *John* by Richard Burridge, and *Proverbs* by Enid Mellor, a former lecturer in religious education at King's College, London.

PBC EXTRACTS

I HAVE SEEN THE LORD!

After Peter and the other disciple have gone home, Mary stays outside the tomb, frozen in her grief (20:11). She has been through the desolation of watching Jesus die on the cross; at least she was there, unlike Peter (19:25). But now she suffers a second grief with the loss of his body. She wanted to weep for him, to have something to hold on to in her pain—but even that has gone.

Messengers in white

Bent double in her agony, she peers into the tomb and sees two figures in white, keeping watch at the head and foot of where Jesus had lain (20:12). John says they are 'angels', which means 'messengers'. Mary is so locked into her tears that she does not realize who they are, since she does not react as people in the Bible usually do when they see angels. She is too wrapped up in her own concerns to be frightened or awe-struck. She just wants to be left alone in her grief. Instead, they question her: 'woman, why are you weeping?' (20:13). On the surface this is a silly thing to ask someone at a grave; the answer is obvious and the question intrusive. Yet at a deeper level, they are right to ask—for if Mary only knew what we know about Jesus, she would be weeping tears of joy. But she replies with almost the same words she told Peter and the beloved disciple (see 20:2). It is the cracked record of a bereaved person, telling the same story over and over and over again, becoming ever more personal; Jesus is now '*my* Lord' and '*I* do not know where they have laid him', not 'we'. Engrossed in her grief, she does not wait for a reply, but turns away.

The gardener?

As she turns around, she becomes aware of someone else standing behind her, whom she was too occupied to notice before; even now she does not recognize that it is the very person she is looking for (20:14). So great is her desire to mourn alone, she looks away again, since she does not face him until he calls her name (20:16). Jesus, too, will not leave her alone, but repeats the angels' question, 'woman, why are you weeping?' For the moment he calls her 'woman', as he did his mother long ago in Cana and from the cross (2:4; 19:26). In another 'echo', he adds the first words he spoke in this gospel, which he repeated to those who came to arrest him in the garden: 'whom are you looking for?' (20:15; see 1:38 and 18:4, 7). Mary misses these allusions and mistakes him for 'the gardener'. Impervious in her grief, she repeats her story; if he has moved the body, 'tell me where you have laid him and I will take him away'. She just wants to find Jesus' body, to hold on to it and grieve in peace. So the cracked record goes round and round and only a miracle will change it. And that is exactly what happens, as Jesus moves from 'woman' to gently whispering her name, 'Mary'. The sheep know their shepherd's voice when 'he calls them by name and leads them out' (10:3). Recognizing the good shepherd's voice, she turns again to face him, 'Rabbouni', my master! (20:16). The heart of this personal encounter with the risen Jesus is encapsulated in those two names, 'Mary', 'Master'. 'They' have not taken him anywhere; there was nothing passive in the passion, and he is still in control now: he has risen from the dead!

A new relationship for a new message

But Mary is still the same, she wants to cling on to him, to possess him as before. Jesus explains that in their new relationship she cannot 'hold on' to the risen Christ. Instead, she has a task, to be the apostle of the resurrection; Jesus sends her to go and tell the news to the disciples who would have met him themselves if only they had not 'gone home'. In this gospel, everyone gets a new task after meeting Jesus, as he brings a new covenant relationship: we are brothers and sisters with Jesus, children of 'my Father and your Father, my God and your God' (20:17; see Lev. 26:12; Jer. 31:33; Ruth 1:16). Having seen God's messenger angels, Mary becomes one herself: she goes *angellousa*, 'announcing' to the disciples how Jesus has replaced her cracked record with a new song: 'I have seen the Lord'— and declaring all the wonders he had told her (20:18).

This is the heart of every Christian's story, that the risen Jesus meets us and calls us out of our selfish concerns to become an angel, announcing to everyone, 'I have seen the Lord'.

Prayer

Lord Jesus, speak through my tears, call me by my name and give me a new song to sing—that you are risen and alive for evermore!

RELATIONSHIPS OF MANY KINDS

These verses, which at first sight look unconnected, have running through them the theme of relationships—within families, with friends, with members of the household, with acquaintances of every kind, and with God.

The family is the setting for verses 1, 2 and 6. 'Feasting with strife' (v. 1) is literally 'sacrifice with strife'. After certain sacrifices, some of the meat was left to be eaten (see 7:14), and this formed the main dish of a feast. However, family celebrations are notoriously stressful! Then as now, such occasions could be noisy and exhausting, and quarrels were likely to arise. It is preferable to eat in peace, even if it means a simple meal, than to be at odds with each other, however elaborate the menu.

In verse 2, the virtues of hard work and the use of intelligence are once again praised. In ancient Israel, a slave was counted as one of the family, and could even become the heir if the master had no son (see Genesis 15:2–3). Where a child brings disgrace on the family, the clever, capable slave can displace that child as an heir after the father's death. The message here is that ability can outrun privilege, even in a social structure where privilege is well-established.

Since, according to Proverbs, long life is the reward for goodness and to have children is a blessing, to live to see our grandchildren (v. 6) brings a special joy—as many grandparents can testify. However, the relationships between the generations need to be good at every level. We approve of children being obedient and well-disciplined—in other words, a credit to their parents. But here it is pointed out that parents also can, and should, bring pleasure and happiness to their children. Family relationships are two-way, and the happiest households are those where each generation is given the appropriate dignity and support.

Wicked talk

It is not only the person who spreads scandal who is guilty; those who listen are equally to blame. Taking notice of wicked talk implies that we are wicked (v. 4); welcoming lies makes us liars (literally 'a walking falsehood'). Evil words will die if they are not well-received, but they flourish in an atmosphere of approval.

Proverbs shows a special concern for the underprivileged. Mocking them (v. 5), like oppressing them, means we insult their—and our—Creator (see 14:31). To enjoy their misfortunes is a form of unkindness that will not go unnoticed or unpunished.

'Fine speech' (v. 7) means something excessive—what we sometimes call 'talking big'. The person who indulges in this is the worst kind of fool (the word appears only three times in Proverbs; here, in v. 21, and at 30:22). To a lack of moral, intellectual and spiritual insight is added an element of boorishness. In 1 Samuel 25:25, Abigail, whose husband is called Nabal, the same word as 'fool', says to David, 'Do not take seriously this ill-natured fellow, Nabal; for as his name is, so is he; Nabal is his name, and folly is with him.'

By contrast, the 'ruler', or 'noble person', has a title to be lived up to, so truthfulness is even more important.

If we want to keep our friends (v. 9), we have to forgive ('cover up' or ignore) hurtful words and thoughtless actions—easier said than done. But to dwell on these upsets does no good either to us or to the friendship.

Effective but wrong

Verse 8 is not about a close relationship, but about a practice which works like a magic stone, or amulet, for the one who offers it. The observation is made here without any moral comment, but elsewhere bribery is firmly forbidden, for example, in Exodus 23:8.

How God sees us

Our relationships with each other are important and we must work at them. But does anyone ever fully know another human being? However we answer, God is the One from whom nothing is hidden (v. 3). Just as precious metals are refined by a physical process in order to reveal their true character, so God alone can make a true estimate of our strengths and weaknesses.

Prayer

Lord, I need help in my relationships with other people, but most of all I need to be right with you.

ADVENT AND LENT

BRF's Advent and Lent books are among the highlights of our publishing year, with well-known authors choosing their own distinctive theme around which they offer daily Bible readings, comment and points for reflection or prayer for every day in Advent and Lent. Material for group use is also included. While our Advent books are published in September, before the Christmas season begins, our Lent titles appear in November so that churches can use them when planning their Lent reading for the following spring.

Recent Lent books include *When They Crucified My Lord* by Brother Ramon SSF, *Faith Odyssey* by Richard Burridge, and *With Jesus in the Upper Room* by David Winter. Among our recent Advent books are *On the Way to Bethlehem* by Hilary McDowell, *A Candle of Hope* by Garth Hewitt, and *The Heart of Christmas* by Chris Leonard.

'SEASONS OF LIFE'

BRF also publishes books of Bible readings for people at different stages of life or in particular circumstances, as part of our regular publishing programme of adult titles. *Never Too Old to Grow* by Alexine Crawford is a book of readings for carers, combining insights from the Bible with stories of personal change and growth, drawn from the experiences of caring for people in the final 'Fourth Age' of life. By contrast, *In the Beginning* by Stephen and Jacqui Hance offers Bible insights for the first weeks of parenting, taking passages from across Scripture and exploring the simple lessons that they teach for this challenging time of life. Among other titles in this range are *Beauty from Ashes* by Jennifer Rees Larcombe (readings for times of loss), *Summer Wisdom* by Eric Rew (reflections from the book of Proverbs) and *The Best is Yet to Be* by Richard Morgan (a book of readings for older people).

HOW TO ORDER BRF NOTES

If you have enjoyed reading this sampler and would like to order the dated notes on a regular basis, they can be obtained through:

CHRISTIAN BOOKSHOPS

Most Christian bookshops stock BRF notes and books. You can place a regular order with your bookshop for yourself or for your church. For details of your nearest stockist please contact the BRF office.

INDIVIDUAL SUBSCRIPTION

For yourself

By placing an annual subscription for BRF notes, you can ensure you will receive your copy regularly. We also send you additional information about BRF: BRF News, Barnabas News, information about our new publications and updates about our ministry activities.

You can also order a subscription for three years (two years for *Day by Day with God*), for an even easier and more economical way to obtain your Bible reading notes.

Gift subscription

Why not give a gift subscription to New Daylight, Guidelines or Day by Day with God to a friend or family member? Simply complete all parts of the order form on the next page and return it to us with your payment. You can even enclose a message for the gift recipient.

For either of the above, please complete the 'Individual Subscription Order Form' and send with your payment to BRF.

CHURCH SUBSCRIPTION

If you order, directly from BRF, five or more copies from our Bible reading notes range of *New Daylight*, *Guidelines* or *Day by Day with God*, they will be sent post-free. This is known as a church subscription and it is a convenient way of bulk-ordering notes for your church. There is no need to send payment with your initial order. Please complete the 'Church Subscriptions Order Form' and we will send you an invoice with your first delivery of notes.

- **Annual subscription:** you can place a subscription for a full year, receiving one invoice for the year. Once you place an annual church subscription, you will be sent the requested number of Bible reading notes automatically. You will also receive useful information to help you run your church group. You can amend your order at any time, as your requirements increase or decrease. Church subscriptions run from May to April of each year. If you start in the middle of a subscription year, you will receive an invoice for the remaining issues of the current subscription year.
- **Standing order:** we can set up a standing order for your Bible reading notes order. Approximately six to seven weeks before a new edition of the notes is due to start, we will process your order and send it with an invoice.

Day by DAY with GOD
BIBLE READINGS FOR WOMEN

PLUS: The New Daylight Magazine
Karen Laister · David Winter
Brother Ramon SSF · Henry Wansbrough

New Daylight

Peter Graves
Rob Gillion
Jenny Robertson
Helen Julian CSF
Jane Cornish
Veronica Zundel
Margaret Cundiff
David Winter
Colin Evans
David Spriggs

Daily readings from

Guidelines
IN-DEPTH BIBLE STUDY

1 Corinthians 1—11
GERALD DOWNING

Esther
KATRINA LARKIN

Lament and Complaint
TREVOR DENNIS

Mark 11—16
JOHN PARR

The Lord's Prayer
IAN WALLIS

1 Corinthians 12—16
GERALD DOWNING

Plus The Guidelines Magazine
Katharine Dell · David Winter · Brother Ramon SSF · Henry Morisley

INDIVIDUAL & GIFT SUBSCRIPTIONS

☐ I would like to give a gift subscription (please complete both name and address sections below)

☐ I would like to take out a subscription myself (complete name and address details only once)

This completed coupon should be sent with appropriate payment to BRF. Alternatively, please write to us quoting your name, address, the subscription you would like for either yourself or a friend (with their name and address), the start date and credit card number, expiry date and signature if paying by credit card.

Gift subscription name _____

Gift subscription address _____

_____

_____ Postcode _____

Please send beginning with the May / September / January issue: *(delete as applicable)*

(please tick box)	UK	SURFACE	AIR MAIL
New Daylight	☐ £10.50	☐ £11.85	☐ £14.10
New Daylight 3-year sub	☐ £26.50		
New Daylight LARGE PRINT	☐ £16.20	☐ £19.80	☐ £24.30
Guidelines	☐ £10.50	☐ £11.85	☐ £14.10
Guidelines 3-year sub	☐ £26.50		
Day by Day with God	☐ £11.55	☐ £12.90	☐ £15.15
Day by Day with God 2-year sub	☐ £19.99		

Please complete the payment details below and send your coupon, with appropriate payment to: BRF, First Floor, Elsfield Hall, 15–17 Elsfield Way, Oxford OX2 8FG.

Your name _____

Your address _____

_____

_____ Postcode _____

Total enclosed £ _____ (cheques should be made payable to 'BRF')

Payment by ☐ cheque   ☐ postal order   ☐ Visa   ☐ Mastercard   ☐ Switch

Card number: ☐☐☐☐☐☐☐☐☐☐☐☐☐☐☐☐☐☐☐

Expiry date of card: ☐☐☐☐   Issue number (Switch): ☐☐☐

Signature _____ Date / /

(essential if paying by credit/Switch card)

SAM0102   BRF is a Registered Charity

CHURCH SUBSCRIPTIONS

Name _____

Address _____

_____

_____ Postcode _____

Telephone Number_____

E-mail _____

Church _____

Denomination _____

Name of Minister _____

Please start my order from Jan/May/Sep* *(delete as applicable)*

I would like to pay annually / receive an invoice each issue of the notes
(delete as applicable)

Please send me:	**Quantity**
New Daylight	_____
New Daylight Large Print	_____
Guidelines	_____
Day by Day with God	_____

Please do not enclose payment. We have a fixed subscription year for Church Subscriptions, which is from May to April each year. If you start a Church Subscription in the middle of a subscription year, we will invoice you for the number of issues remaining in that year.

PBC ORDER FORM

Please ensure that you complete and send off both sides of this order form.

Please send me the following book(s):

	Qty	Price	Total
030 8 PBC: 1 & 2 Samuel (H. Mowvley)	_____	£7.99	_____
118 5 PBC: 1 & 2 Kings (S. Dawes)	_____	£7.99	_____
070 7 PBC: Chronicles—Nehemiah (M. Tunnicliffe)	_____	£7.99	_____
031 6 PBC: Psalms 1—72 (D. Coggan)	_____	£7.99	_____
065 0 PBC: Psalms 73—150 (D. Coggan)	_____	£7.99	_____
071 5 PBC: Proverbs (E. Mellor)	_____	£7.99	_____
087 1 PBC: Jeremiah (R. Mason)	_____	£7.99	_____
028 6 PBC: Nahum—Malachi (G. Emmerson)	_____	£7.99	_____
191 6 PBC: Matthew (J. Proctor)	_____	£7.99	_____
046 4 PBC: Mark (D. France)	_____	£7.99	_____
027 8 PBC: Luke (H. Wansbrough)	_____	£7.99	_____
029 4 PBC: John (R.A. Burridge)	_____	£7.99	_____
082 0 PBC: Romans (J. Dunn)	_____	£7.99	_____
122 3 PBC: 1 Corinthians (J. Murphy-O'Connor)	_____	£7.99	_____
073 1 PBC: 2 Corinthians (A. Besançon Spencer)	_____	£7.99	_____
012 X PBC: Galatians and 1 & 2 Thessalonians (J. Fenton)	_____	£7.99	_____
047 2 PBC: Ephesians—Colossians & Philemon (M. Maxwell)	_____	£7.99	_____
119 3 PBC: Timothy, Titus and Hebrews (D. France)	_____	£7.99	_____
092 8 PBC: James—Jude (F. Moloney)	_____	£7.99	_____
3297 5 PBC: Revelation (M. Maxwell)	_____	£7.99	_____

Total cost of books £ _____

Postage and packing (see over) £ _____

TOTAL £ _____

Please complete the payment details below and send your coupon, with appropriate payment to: BRF, First Floor, Elsfield Hall, 15—17 Elsfield Way, Oxford OX2 8FG.

Your name _____

Your address _____

_____

_____ Postcode _____

Total enclosed £ _____ (cheques should be made payable to 'BRF')

Payment by ☐ cheque   ☐ postal order   ☐ Visa   ☐ Mastercard   ☐ Switch

Card number: ☐☐☐☐ ☐☐☐☐ ☐☐☐☐ ☐☐☐☐ ☐☐☐☐ ☐☐☐☐

Expiry date of card: ☐☐☐☐   Issue number (Switch): ☐☐☐

Signature _____ Date   /   /

(essential if paying by credit/Switch card)

SAM0102

BRF is a Registered Charity

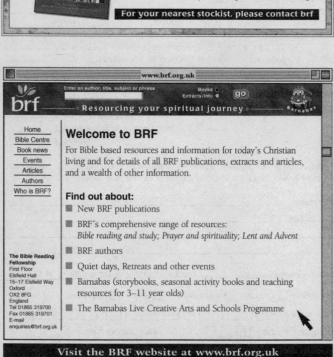